No Lex 10-12

Famous Explorers

Francisco Pizarro

Jeff
Donaldson-Forbes

The Rosen Publishing Group's
PowerKids Press™
New York

To Isabella Luz Octaviano

Published in 2002 by The Rosen Publishing Group, Inc.
29 East 21st Street, New York, NY 10010

Copyright © 2002 by The Rosen Publishing Group, Inc.

First Edition

Book Design: Maria E. Melendez and Felicity Erwin

Project Editor: Kathy Campbell

Photo Credits: pp. 4 (background), p 4 (inset), 8, 9, 11, 15, 19 (foreground), 19 (Atahuallpa) © North Wind Pictures;. pp. 7 (Incan objects), 7 (inset) © SuperStock; pp. 16 (top), 16 (center), 16 (bottom), 20 © The Granger Collection.

Donaldson-Forbes, Jeff.
   Francisco Pizarro / Jeff Donaldson-Forbes.—1st ed.
      p. cm. — (Famous explorers)
   ISBN 0-8239-5831-0 (lib. bdg.)
1. Pizarro, Francisco, ca. 1475–1541—Juvenile literature. 2. Peru—History—Conquest, 1522–1548—Juvenile literature.
3. South America—Discovery and exploration—Spanish—Juvenile literature. 4. Explorers—Peru—Biography—Juvenile literature.
5. Explorers—Spain—Biography—Juvenile literature. I. Title. II. Series.
F3442.7.P776 D66 2001
985'.02'092—dc21
                                                                                              00-011109

Manufactured in the United States of America

Contents

4

A Young Soldier

There are no records of Francisco Pizarro's birth, but most historians believe he was born in 1471. He was born in the town of Trujillo, Spain. His father and mother were not married. Pizarro never attended school and he never learned to read or write.

During Pizarro's youth, **explorers** like Christopher Columbus were discovering new lands across the Atlantic Ocean. The explorers were meeting Native Americans for the first time. The Catholic Church hoped to **convert** the native people to the Christian religion.

When he was a teenager, Pizarro joined the Spanish army. He spent his whole life as a soldier. The army taught Pizarro to fight without fear. Spanish soldiers were famous for their courage. They were not afraid to die fighting for what they believed.

Far left: *This picture shows Pizarro as a soldier. Although his father was a captain in the army, Francisco had no contact with him after he was born.*
Top: *This drawing from the early 1500s shows a Spanish harquebusier, a type of soldier who fires a heavy gun that needs a special support.*

The Incas

During the 1200s, in the part of South America that is today's Peru, a group of Native Americans began building a great **civilization**. These people would later be called the Incas. The word *Inca* comes from the name of the ruler, whom the Native Americans called the Inca. The Incas fought other groups of Native Americans to capture their land. Besides being warriors, the Incas were also farmers, **engineers**, and artists. They built giant stepped **pyramids** and created **irrigation** systems to water their crops. They had their own religion. They believed in many different gods.

Before Spaniards met the Incas, other Native Americans told the soldiers stories of great cities built of gold. The Spaniards were greedy for gold that would make them rich in their own country. Wherever they found gold, they stole it and sent it home to Spain.

These ruins of a temple near Pisco, Peru, show how Incan engineers placed stone blocks without using any material to join the blocks. Incan artists created beautiful gold and silver jewelry, such as the pieces seen here, and even large plates that were used to cover the walls of rooms.

Hispaniola

Pizarro's Travels

Pizarro's life as a Spanish soldier took him far away from Spain. When he was in his 20s and 30s, Pizarro traveled to the island of Hispaniola in the Caribbean Sea. He also went to Colombia in South America.

In 1513, Pizarro traveled with a Spanish explorer named Balboa. Native Americans near what is now known as Panama had told Balboa about a great ocean on the western coast of South America. No Spaniards had ever seen the ocean, and Balboa was determined to find it. On September 25, 1513, Balboa's **expedition** climbed a mountain that was high enough to let them see the Pacific Ocean. Pizarro was now seeing the ocean that would become an important part of his life.

Balboa discovers the Pacific Ocean.

This map from the 1600s is printed in Latin and shows the island of Hispaniola (today's Haiti and Dominican Republic) and the continent of South America. In 1502, Pizarro sailed across the Atlantic Ocean for the first time. He went to Hispaniola.

9

Pizarro's Plans

Pizarro was rewarded for his service to the Spanish army. Around 1522, he became the mayor of Panama, a city south of Mexico. Pizarro was about 51 years old, but he knew there were many places farther south that the Spaniards had not explored, along the western coast of South America. He began planning a trip to the south with two other men. One man was Diego de Almagro, a Spanish soldier. The other man, Hernando de Luque, was a priest who wanted to convert Native Americans to Christianity. Luque agreed to raise money for the expedition. Almagro **recruited** and trained soldiers for the trip. Pizarro led the expedition. He made an agreement with the other two men. The land that they **conquered** during the trip and all of the treasure that they brought back would be split equally among the three men.

By 1522, Pizarro (seen here) was fairly rich as mayor of Panama. He started to see himself as a conquistador. A conquistador is a leader in the Spanish conquest of the Americas.

Francisco Pizarro

Caribbean Sea

ATLANTIC OCEAN

PANAMA
Panama City

VENEZUELA

COLOMBIA

GUYANA
FRENCH GUIANA
SURINAME

1524 ■ Expedition 1
1526–28 ■ Expedition 2
1531–33 ■ Expedition 3
Gallo Island

Quito
ECUADOR

Equator

Tumbes
PERÚ

BRAZIL

San Miguel (Piura)
Cajamarca

SOUTH AMERICA

INCA EMPIRE
Lima (Founded 1535)
Cuzco

PACIFIC OCEAN

BOLIVIA

PARAGUAY

CHILE

URUGUAY

ARGENTINA

The First and Second Expeditions

In 1524, Pizarro sailed south from Panama with a crew of about 100 men aboard two ships. The trip was a terrible one. Rough weather and sickness killed many of the men even before they landed. So many men died of starvation that they named the place where they camped Puerto de la Hambre, or Hungry Harbor. They were forced to return to Panama. In 1526, Pizarro tried the trip again. He got as far as Tumbes, a city on the Pacific coast of what is today Peru. In Tumbes, the Native Americans treated Pizarro's men kindly. They showed the Spaniards their temples of silver and gold. Pizarro was careful to treat these people with respect. He knew that he did not have enough men with him to steal such treasures. Pizarro and his men again returned to Panama.

Pizarro's two trips prepared him for what he must do next. He had to recruit a large army and prepare them to travel by land and by sea. With enough men, Pizarro believed he could conquer Tumbes and claim the land and the gold for Spain.

By Sea and by Land

To recruit a large Spanish army, Pizarro needed permission from Emperor Charles V in Spain. In 1528, Pizarro sailed from Panama to Spain to ask Charles V for permission to form a Spanish army and take it to South America. Emperor Charles V agreed to let Pizarro recruit 250 men. Pizarro was allowed to conquer Incan lands in the name of Spain. Emperor Charles V ordered Pizarro to take priests on the journey to convert the Native Americans.

Pizarro left Spain with 180 men in January 1530 and returned to Panama to train his army. In January 1531, they sailed south in three ships toward Peru. After two weeks of bad weather, they decided to travel by land. They left the ships in the Bay of San Mateo. From there they headed toward Tumbes, riding the horses they had brought with them.

Top: In 1528, Pizarro spoke before Charles V in Spain, asking him for permission to form an army to explore South America. Bottom: Pizarro and his men had to lead their horses up the Andes Mountains in northern Peru.

The Spaniards stole gold jewelry, like this pair of gold ear ornaments, from the Native Americans.

This gold figure from the first to third centuries probably was used as an ornament by Native Americans in Peru.

Peruvian artists in the 1400s made gold masks like this one to fit over the faces of people who died.

Pizarro Meets the Incas

Pizarro's army began traveling by land north of Tumbes. On the way, the Spaniards met many Native Americans. Sometimes these people were friendly and welcomed the Spaniards. Other times they attacked Pizarro's army with poison arrows. Wherever they traveled, the Spaniards stole gold and silver. Their greed was never satisfied. They believed that these precious metals would make each of them very powerful back home. They returned to their boats and loaded them with the stolen treasure.

At this time, the Incas were fighting a **civil war**. The war had pitted Incas against one another, weakening the empire. On November 15, 1532, Pizarro's army arrived in the valley of Cajamarca in northern Peru. The Incan ruler, Atahuallpa, was camped in this town. An enormous Incan army waited for Pizarro and his men.

A Great Conflict

Atahuallpa sent messengers to greet Pizarro's army. One messenger brought gifts. Another asked Pizarro to turn back. Pizarro's men advanced into the valley and through the gates of the city of Cajamarca. They marched through an empty city, though. Most of the Incas were in hiding, or camping in the hills outside the city. Pizarro sent two soldiers to speak with Atahuallpa and to invite him to have dinner with Pizarro. Atahuallpa agreed to dine with Pizarro the next evening. Pizarro expected Atahuallpa to lead the Incas back into the city. He planned to hide his soldiers and attack the Incas once they were inside the city. The next night, Atahuallpa stopped outside the city gates. Through messengers, Pizarro assured Atahuallpa that there was nothing to fear. Atahuallpa decided to enter the city of Cajamarca.

Top left: Atahuallpa was the thirteenth and last ruler of the Incas. Top right: This picture of Pizarro from 1598 shows him as a respected explorer.

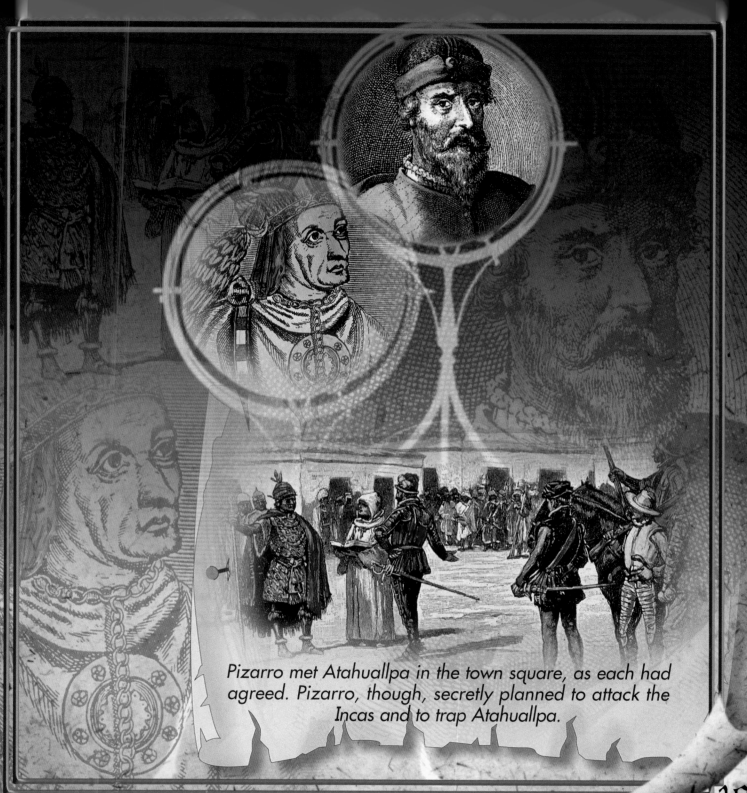

Pizarro met Atahuallpa in the town square, as each had agreed. Pizarro, though, secretly planned to attack the Incas and to trap Atahuallpa.

19

Atahuallpa

A Deadly Battle

Pizarro gave a signal and his men attacked the Incas. The Incas were unprepared. They could not defend themselves against the Spaniards. Pizarro's men fought with swords, cannons, and crossbows. The Incas fought with clubs and arrows. The Incas were scared of the Spanish horses. The Incas had never seen horses before. Many Incas believed that the horse and the soldier riding it were one creature! The Spaniards trampled the Incas with their horses and killed thousands. None of Pizarro's men lost their lives. Atahuallpa was taken prisoner for nine months. He offered a **ransom** for his freedom. Pizarro agreed to the offer. Atahuallpa ordered his servants to fill a room with gold and silver. After the servants filled the room with treasure, they expected their ruler to be freed. Instead, Pizarro had Atahuallpa killed in August 1533.

Pizarro never meant to keep his word to Atahuallpa, the Incan ruler, and had him killed in August 1533.

A Bloody End

In 1535, Pizarro took control of the Incan capital city, Cuzco. He fought his partner Almagro for control of Cuzco. In July 1538, Pizarro had Almagro killed. Pizarro ruled the entire Incan Empire from a palace in Lima, a city that he had built in Peru. He lived the rest of his life surrounded by the treasures he had stolen. In Spain, Emperor Charles V heard about Pizarro's evil deeds. Charles V ordered Pizarro to be stripped of his titles and wealth. On July 26, 1541, supporters of Almagro killed Pizarro in his palace. It was a bloody end to the violent life of Francisco Pizarro. He will be remembered for his **encounter** with the Incan civilization. Sadly, he also will be known for destroying it.

Pizarro's Timeline

1471	Probable year of Pizarro's birth in Trujillo, Spain.
1502	He arrives in Hispaniola.
1522	He is named mayor of Panama.
1524–26	He makes two voyages along the west coast of South America. He visits the city of Tumbes, Peru.
1532	Pizarro arrives in Cajamarca.
1533	The Incan ruler Atahuallpa is killed.
1541	Pizarro is killed.

Glossary

civil war (SIH-vul WOR) A war between two sides within one country.

civilization (sih-vih-lih-ZAY-shun) A group of people living in an organized and similar way.

conquered (KON-kerd) To have overcome or gotten the better of something.

convert (kuhn-VERT) To change religious beliefs.

encounter (in-KOWN-ter) To meet someone or something by chance. An encounter also can be a meeting in battle.

engineers (en-jih-NEERZ) People who are experts at planning and building engines, machines, roads, bridges, and canals.

expedition (ek-spuh-DIH-shun) A trip for a special purpose such as scientific study.

explorers (ik-SPLOR-urz) People who travel to different places to learn more about them.

irrigation (ih-rih-GAY-shun) To carry water to land through ditches or pipes.

pyramids (PEER-uh-mids) Large stone structures with square bottoms and triangular sides that meet at a point on top.

ransom (RAN-sum) A price paid or demanded before a captured person or prisoner is set free.

recruited (ree-KROOT-ed) To have gotten people to join an army.

Index

Web Sites

To learn more about Francisco Pizarro, check out these Web sites:
http://www.encarta.msn.com/reference
http://www.comptons.com/encyclopedia